MW00323991

The Louder the Room the Darker the Screen

Paul Ebenkamp

Oakland, California 2015

2015 Creative Commons BY-SA
Paul Ebenkamp

Timeless, Infinite Light

at Omni Commons
4799 Shattuck Avenue
Oakland, CA 94609

ISBN 978-1-937421-09-0

First Edition

Printed by Litho Books and 1984 Printing

Distributed by Small Press Distribution

Some of these poems have appeared in *The Equalizer,*
Where Eagles Dare, Calaveras, Dusie, Cultural Society,
SFMOMA Open Space, Macaroni Necklace, and *Try!.*

timelessinfinitelight.com

The meaning of windows is air.

—Gertrude Stein

Hell is Now Love

"given the right woods"
gain knob twisting
on its own time
between thumb and index
and pool and ashpit
carved at distances
about you
are that thing
within a radius
void and fluttering
twined rope around
itself by holding still
inside the push
my knocked-out
wind made
when space leaned in
"an odor, a chime"
of rivers of wires
and sun a hole sunk

in the 3D scenery's
torqued and
bell-clear blacklight
some ways back
sudden flash
and hungered
from the depths
of a bloodclot
still teething what
the mouth rounds up
on a playground
drift into wordy
years of not
leaving the office
\\\\\\\\\\\\\\\\\\\\\\\\\\\\\\
/////////// as in the wide
going down of day
into serrated dew
grounds gnaw
the dazzling walls
"I fly, my dust
will be what I am"
in dark grass
behind festival
fencing whence
a head's pestered
with identities
and mind's bad
aim it grieves
the heavens

to see it only
breathe to refute the air
trim blocks of
no future ago
where the doom
metal riff ends
in circular sundown
the rhythm thinning
as it nears the shore
and one is waved on
absolved from all
in-flight entertainment
and so sat screaming
in quiet
wherein a name is
only the changes it's
subject to but
cannot aim at
as if living weren't
a fact but rather
a bearing so rare
in brick that nothing
could distract it \\\\\\\
/////////////////////////////
\\\\\\\\\\\\\\\\\\\\\ or out
here on the other
side of either way
as I'm *telos*-lapped
by a DDoS attack
wherein the line is

busy every countless
night I've tried
to write its names
down for the first time
in crystal-thin liquid
the chamber square
darkens then an azure
cringe of centered
death or whatever gets
you in the doorframe
blanking thinkfully
to a video of eight
hours of rain
limning into why is
it we're seated at
such day jobs square-
pushing up against
a basis in nature
and the pressing
question of so do
you just get your
guesswork wherever
The Perished
Patterns murmur
as our time here
is tap water drawn
through glass so thick
it hurts my eyes
to even think about it
astride environs

of ardor and nerve
whose gully's lousy
with woodland beasts
who aerate dirt
by burying seed
forgetting where
and yielding trees
through cordless
and waste skies
the big dream
flinching in its
unctuous mayhem
up and down and
up the drain \\\\\\\\\
/////////////////////////////
\\\\\\\\\\\\\\\\\\\\\\\\\\\\\\
/////////////// but no one
knows what happens
when a song ends
somewhere in the
mileage between
sine wave and scale
a drone without
first or last grain
accrues in you
and isn't a visitor
less than its senses
its lust and expense
so wrote it as might
keep the derelict

abandon all hope
who enter here
let day and night
go leave day
and night alone
enough is too much
and when to rest
from lasting
is the point
or else what do you
expect's to be left of
us but laminated
ashes and compound
fracture concentrate
and piles of spent
adhesive strata pried
from the backside
of habitus braced by
its hated adjectives
for the big reveal
its green accountant
visor peppered with clues
out of which with
pastels I encroach
thinking overmuch
within arm's
reach of sustenance
runs at the heart
chewed shadow
"in another ether"

it's Stevens-y noonbreak
my goodness how
the dust settles without
stinginess on iced-
over winter lawn
grass crashing
underfoot to pull
the clouds down
and icons knocked
around an exact
room of you ////////
\\\\\\\\\\\\\\\\\\\\\\\\\
/////////////////////////
\\\\\\\\\\\\\\\\\\\\\\\\
/////////////////////////
\\\\\\\ and sure hell
might be love now
but what isn't
one worth turns
into another as
I gathered on
returning from
what followed
us into its clingy
entropy that there
are hours
that night
in this hemisphere
devotes solely
to the Pacific ocean

and fell into
a prayer of
you are hovering
ten feet above the
surface of it
you look down
and through
unchanging
states fell \\\\\\\\\\\\\\\\\\\\
/////////////////////////////////////
\\\\\\\\\\\\\\\ O cinerescence
O cirrus on tin
and not a word of sleep
as the brevity of life
loomed madly
in the corridor of days
cast gladly out
not even almost what it is
as if some manner
of draft flesh with
its face on backwards
past jigsaw aspects
feeling which
end's which
in that sap held
a child tired of feeding
who could not know
if acts were natural
running unassuaged
through skeletized fields

their redundant
bumper crops
blinking through
the allergens
the whole mess
reducible
to two cassettes
whether corrosion
or ornament
there's no telling
\\\\\\\\\\\\\\\\\\\\\\\\\\\
/////////////////////////////
\\\\\\\\\\\\\\\\\\\\\\\\\\\\
//////// and if another
being becomes
me in its hearsay
passing through
a boondocks silo's
worth of psyche
from practice back
to habit back
to accident
"where the firing
squad has
nothing to aim at"
but the genitals
hanging by a thread
from an off-screen
prop body in the
Empyreanic

fractal fish-eyed
Busby Berkeley
choreography
surrounding you
with powder and
smoking bowls
of gemstones
they're smoking bowls
of precious metals
and cutting up
the pieces looking
busy in a travesty
of foregroundless
contour and back-
groundless relief
the tale pertains
mostly to the time
it takes to tell it
With Midnight
to the North
of Her / And
Midnight to the
South of Her
/////////////////////////
\\\\\\\\\\\\\\\\\\\\\\\\\\\\\
/////////////////////////
\\\\\\\\\\\\\\\\\\\\\\\\\\\\\
///////////////////////
\\\\\\\\\\\\\\\\\\\\\\\\\\
hot autumn today

clever in its waves
that don't crash
the scoreless
innings that brush by
where were the barriers
that worried me
dowsing adjacencies
in framed things
nothing rains down
as a web between
the eyes of what's
within is still except us
or spelling just
isn't in this alphabet
of old stars
outside screaming
ACCELERATE!
and have sung
to the slowed ones
for eons once
it was lace scrap
oozed from the intercom
my thumb could double
every consonant
until the hurtful
words don't work
by method going dead
with error for more
pneumatic upswing
and stations lining

up outside the sky
to listen like a mouth
if whatever is is bound
to be a little off
and nothing only
comes to so much
however elsewhere
the known goes
a swollen alloy
ends in keening
oily at dawn and
drills to the kernel
stray of repair as
specialties totter
on and everything
is fire

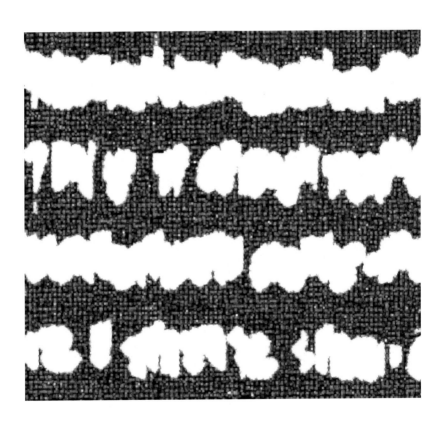

Long Time Listener, First Time Caller

Useful worthlessness!, like an iota outside it
's just the socket holds the wall that way. Listen,

I saw a nature documentary about nature in general called
Of Everything Only an Infinitesimal Sliver's Not Elsewhere,

inset with kneecaps shattered by an email—these are the risks
we take.
Wake up!

It's Tuesday, I don't know what day it is, hold that thought, on second thought don't—

Light dilates here and can contract somewhere else.
Walk us through it, the audience begs the dreaming speech.

I'm calling to request a hex on whatever it was hid the myriads!
O pluck me from this haze of spellcheck!

It seemed from the program that nature's whole message was
DIE OFTEN.
This was still the mirror stage.

Are lungs considered guts?
Is an ear a digit or a limb?

Rain fell wherever.
Here's 'em some soft punk support:

May my mind vanish as you open my mouth!

And on into volume, standing with traffic, fused to the present
but not to its tense, in allowance and effort's sanguine lack;

there may be lots to toggle back
and forth about
but come to think of it.

"Though the species is in me, I am neutral."
Such flex!

SWORN OUT OF
SECRECY AND INTO
THE LIKELIHOOD
OF BEING STUCK IN
DIRT AND MADE TO
BURST LIKE TALK
INTO WHAT NEVER
ARRIVES AND NEVER
LEAVES, SHAPE OR
JUST INCLINATION
MAYBE, AN OCTAVE,
POEM BETWEEN POEM

THIS NOTCH
IN THE
SAW THIS
SLANT IN
THE HAND

The Unavailable Memory of

▽

You, your attention

subdivided
by the testcard

called "Dust Rises From Highways"—

∞

You whose
generally pretty leaden
programming of a sudden cuts
clear of itself, in an odd gust—

✳

You, a mostly empty set

whose channels
may be changed

though they weigh a distant ton—

SENSE-
LESS
UNDER
COATS
OF FOCUS

CAN'T THINK WITH MY GOOD HAND TIED UP LIKE THIS

Warrant

Witless, not to
think the true
way was?
Before an errant
head's sore lust
I swore, lashed
down, dimmed open—
in other nerves
I'm trying not
that consciousness,
those notices,
harangue me off
the old news of how-
not-to-stay-the-same;
only so an oversought
heart'd know it's going
on. —Two rooms

marooned at each
other's crazed ingress,
indigent as a window
withers what it looks
to: more blood, less
monologue (to be
discontinued into
which, boom-hiss,
this *estranging haste*
neither earth refuses
of us just up
and "goes social"?)!
I heard about it as if
from the knowledgeable:
sudden fuss of rude
resplendence against
a tether's indifference—
the body not even
present enough
to realize what about,
and left to stop
or stand on end so
I'm not positive.

(I–I–I–I–I goes the body clock)

What else one does nothing
to is all; what'll I tell people?

Love and trust to little faith
the slow, weary, exilic waste
stared careless past, ripped
from rest to relic and back,—
a jewel of the sweet lisp
in green doom ringing
clear of which sound
is it the end? —Now *that's*
what I call anything
in sight! Or maybe half of
both worlds, new and duly
unbeautiful: throwing total
fits instead of art, all ears
to the obdurate halcyon I couldn't
think around, craved melee, grew
bemused that there's no secret;
it just rings, a bleached
impudent under more sun...
Pending fluencies the greyscale
follows to resolve into grassland,
these gouges of soft response,
no lost ball, no head's guess
left except one epiphanic doubt:
what's said is meant instead, what's
unsaid instead's what's meant
until these mithering,
grace-forsaken commands
become what's to be touched from:

a what-am-I-thinking-of clip
for the singing
thing to go in. With all the new
misuses jinxed in drivel,
insult and mesmeric
shufflings past, a concussive
breeze flows plain as day;
had I said so, mute as what the curse
cranked up was—?, as if inspired
answers cued a sycophantic rage.

HI TO THE FIREWALL
CROSSING ITSELF
OUT WHILE BLAKE
PLAYED BLACK
METAL BACKWARDS
TO A COMPANY CROWD
FUNNELING TO NUMB-
ER-ADDLED NESS-
LESSNESS'S SENES-
CENCE AND NO
MORE MESSAGES

LESS-
NESS-
LESS-
NESS

The World Company of Lawrence, Kansas

Here, flailing in
perfect orbit the
world's afforded
what it's cost us:

widow channels
back up across
what they cancel,
first-vintage-first-

glitch where the
book blurs shut;
where may returning
all to robo-

call exhaust the
conjurer, as amps
crave wakefulness,
and in between

its doubled notes
may thrash these
data-stabbed white-
outs of eyes high

beyond aura and
obstacle, redial
elided— Begins
with machines

will bring us closer
as a stump hulked
inside the cord,
impediments urged

to sing through
the snarl of rooms
purse like leaves
from a seed— A tic

of ethic to this, one
world veils the
next until another,
soon, arriving

in a hatch pattern
that wants to beam
to you blooms and
turns its back,

remote as the ritual
window through
which there's
just glass. A life

happens again
and that is enough
to unlearn which
events come to

pass, until those
that don't start
to catch— In the
shape of the world

whose occasions
relapse, I can
meander mind
in hand around

the picky darkness
until, funded and
culminating, a language-
long cry of insolvent

attention's sent
dissembling into
dirt like cursive
in the permanent

air, wild above
waste and scale—
And takes to raving
in the killed mirror

we'd used to rake
our moods across
their mind— Throbs,
a throne to go

flagrant in— Sirens
and thickly lined
sums— All to avoid
coarse chores of

one's business, how
to shamble a way
through the day's
ills folding over and/

or over, forgetfully
itself? The world comes
with company, no
problem there, since

reason's already such
a purchase: you can
shiver wherever
the sun is and raise

yourself and never rise.
Oh rest is complex but
it trusts us to be these
imaginary brackets on

that cloud no single
count is right about!
It takes time, I meant
to invent another good

way in— But how auto-
matic's the way back to
the actual? As I grow
fleshed out with verbiage—

Arable, irreparable,
name-and-number-
checked by landfill
services whose

peregrinations slave
a kind of rainfall
down my street,
which with feckless

alacrity never ends—
A paid and paying body,
having said all the
preceding, however

errant, however
ungarrulous, only totally
reforms— Then dead
to, then livid in, then

pixel-dregged,
then shown nothing
but noise under
moneyed shade,

shade that is the
subject of this work,
shade that petrifies
outside the flood

lights, about to
found a company in
its figureheaded
haste to get it fated

and straight before
the seams show. It's
time to change states.
Follow the bouncing

ball trapdoorwards
there at forever's end,
gnomic things turning
until no one's exempt

from the telling of time,
the nerve it takes
to sound it through
so that no one isn't

thinking *it's too loud*
in here for it not to
be cold out, in cases
traceable to everyone;

what the rush is starts
somewhere almost
perfectly as unrelated
as known, our world

occurring not to listen
but to walk through
as the wait time takes
up the whole room—

IT
IS NOT
THE
LAW

Twine Strung From Ear to Ear:
or, I Do Not Blame the World Company

The entertainment involved
in contemporary life
is very persuasive.

True enough, and I'd like
to add to that my menacing
motif, the one with noises.

Or now there's nothing
to say so what's to stop
me from not talking?

To have as direct
as possible an
experience of things?

There are one too many
of us in this area
and I'm glad that one is me.

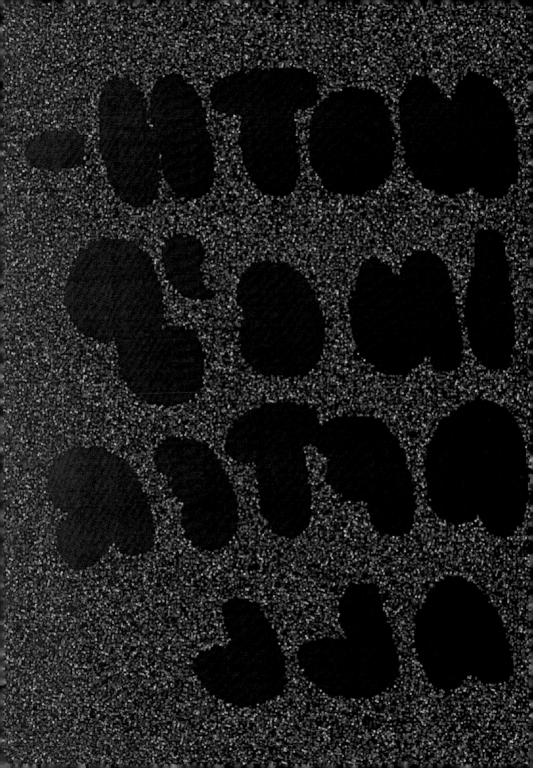

The Animist

That amber

would turn

on fossil

was obvious,

thought I from

an income

concussion

across proper

channels;

looking

down silken

inlets I found

a law to

the worsening

dream:

a matter

of timing

scattered

tightly into

vast blanks that

became seams.

Liberation's

agon, paroxysm

for a glimpse,

another line from Dante,

maybe; the past

is madness it

goes, says, the hour

appearing unreal...

The chorus revolts

in cornflower

blue and silk grey

as what syntax

that thinks it

describes this

dissolves and is

the summer sun

again, horizon

in its cirrus

sleeve, untorn

tissue and cartilage

chiming in on

laminal dawns

half a mind away—

I am at a loss,

but which?

And while you're

on the line

with that hand

in the air,

blood coming

through the storm

screen, it's

great to take

ages to say

what all exists,

because fuck

time's appetites,

we're always

being made

to wait for

more bottled

water to arrive

in the drunk

tank, keeping

us up at all

hours between

the future and

whatever's

happening

now, thrashing

through channels

the world

under, still

calling back

for more of

that music we

were sold by

the hold music

people,

impoverishers,

so that now only

no one's own

hand's shaped

such gusts of

runoff from

the before/

after factory

where, instead

of difference,

there's area:

the subject/object

ratio radiant

like fluoride

in a writer's mouth,

its songs already

almost partly

and not sung,

among burdens

the lifting of

which is their

reason for

falling so solidly

on all sides...

Consonants

watch. It's

been dawn

ever since.

Bind down

and bound

through us,

oh pagan

metal angels

in effigy, among

which grew

ways a body's

open nest

could blast

past its own

fabrication—

"I knew then

what I know

now, namely:

there never

was a time

I couldn't say

just that." And yet

I went and turned

the same again.

Years later harping

often on it. There's

hieroglyphic fog

outside tonight

and in it, using

breath to speak,

a silhouetted

hollow of

accomplishment's

lost and, being

also unsought,

is nowhere

and nowhere

else. Remaining

leaves. Where-

from the warm

jets? I wish

now to conflate

intro with index

and otherwise

get the work done:

all my relations,

your oblivious

and increasing

happinesses,

no need to act

the restless,

decadent,

and generally

blurry courier

stuck dusting

hindsightwise

for heaven's buried

deed; oh I like

to look alive

as some such

surface, what

we cut up,

sprouts half

the time this

is taking away—

For Alli Warren

THIS KNOT,
THAT REF-
RACTS THIS

FILED DOWN
DIGIT THAT
DILATES THIS

PRISM THAT
DIMS BEFORE
THE FLOOD-
LIGHTS THIS

VOICEOVER CLACKING ITS TEETH ON THE MICRO-PHONE GLASS,

Antipode and Bad Math

oblivion's a cutting foam
from where I might see
the slick hitch and pivot of
benevolent neglect's dream
a swarm of polarized iron
drifting through slits in its lid
a body nodding godlessly off
across thought's losses like
plastic atomized in blood
I'm calling through the gush
of fax noise reddening
the wind through the weather
patterns of Planet Assonance
aswim in pineal glands
wherein I sat and sounded out
dark arguments against just
tossing a million ellipses in
between unequal things

heat to vacuum
lacuna to bruise
feeling audile like a surface wave
a hyphen in live vapor
its skin in dehiscence thrown
out or away or strewn on the lawn
rain tapping its membrane
keeping time out of it
a dot between arcs
among which these overly
lineated interstices might
hear rains falling so far from
their season that I rewrite
the calendar to reflect them
stranded as I am
up at headquarters
astride a ladder's steps
its suction cups come unstuck
so the only living thing
to do is keep breathing
four feet out in front of me
until it sickens
the nearest distance's
bare maximum crammed
into prismatic miasma
by which I mean
a bunch of useless
ballast facts flopping
through a lifetime
of entire afternoons

boarded over bland or
rancid in the groaning sum
of all this ink can speechless feel
without a second tongue
holding its shift keys down
on a moon's worth of wattage
to practice my cursive
knee deep in acoustics
but lately food fakes itself
just to get in my mouth
and all I see
beyond these walls
is a lot of paste
not a grace note in sight
the red bulb digits sung
as crazes close over us
as names last an instant
there are no two things
time's just an example
to the time around it
blushing like a thickener
in my skull's guts
whose aura or core is a light
in which I am never shown anything
whose inner ear could sleep
on a freeway median
drunk on background radiation
under the din-bleached sky
bleating down for miles
without internet

SURF DROVE
TINNY NERVE
SHORES FORTH
MOLTEN OMENS
PAPER OVER
DEAD AIR
DEAR CALLER
who can't think it over
whose song's gone lossy
as an MP3 left bleeding
at 96 kilobytes per second
on a ghost beach
coveted for its real estate
and minded like a revenant
any pliant bit of sequoia
bark could have started
(you can hear its knots tie
tighter by reciting the official
line on our surroundings
phoning its performance in
traces of the "anthropic
principle" which from lyric's
waste and waste's
abatement cannot be erased)
its ratio of voice to throat
curtaining between me
heartless marvels depending
a mile above *that* wave out
there at *that* distance

that inch of sifted element
that refracts on contact
with the saturated anima
roaming my chromatic scales
rest after rest after rest
after rest after rest after
which numb clothes like
what we wore to bed become
as studious as shadows
folded open all golden
as by an alphabet's
hex cold protein
rains on hearts of palm
in forts and yards
cascades and acres
dim crests spilling zilch
there's too much to show for it
there's no clouds in the storm
I still can't see a thing in
but remember how light
and edge weren't the same then
and cursive script leaving cursive
stains across the climate
won't sop up that lack
clot with a hole sworn through it
the Great Pacific Garbage Patch
a hissing salvage whorl
whose body's prosody
curdles its surplus
as if nature's heaven

meant zero degrees Kelvin
and we were the silken
awfulness of poesis secreted
from a riot of sand and rock salt
enriching what it conceals
may I be arrayed in a way
that makes more sense
the more I'm detonated
into something else
then fed to the ambience
its habitable neither
and nescient decrement
taking ice apart as light
and dark blue pink orange
purple red yellow and gray
by an asymptote's shoves
I am impossibly unsurrounded
in solvent and octave
soaked fields clanging
the opposite of deletion

For Richard O. Moore

I WAS
envious
of fair
of
REALIST

HOW WE PULLED
IT BLOOD UP
ROM CARTRIDGE
DUST WHILE
BIRDS CHIRPED
AS THE SKIN
WAS TUCKED
CAREFULLY

REPENT

REPEATS

TURGID

TURGID

ORDEALS

REPENT

Carp (After Christopher Wool)

Can't get my head around
to it without caking; it's my treat
to be viewed again, in your mirror.
I used to live several whiles from here
on out since things I know you know
have changed... Now (blush on the dim,
soap in the dust) I watch our star-
of-program pucker in the fly-by-night
extrusions; this is nobody's snow.
Can't believe I stayed wherever I was
ill-sated but for color, curdles in fur,
pursed in a puddle of sap. Haven't
you done enough damage already?
Getting nowhere's plenty. Make me.

Scorcher

Head to the air,
sitting there

an hour from now.
What's afterthought?

FINISH WHAT YOU'VE

CORNER,
BORDER,
CORE, ETC.

LOSS
OF ALL
PAST
PHRASES

COMPULSION, HU-
NGER, OPTIC ST-
RAIN, FORESHO-
RTENING'S FUR-
THERANCES, THE
RHYTHM IN ITS
BRILLIANT GRAYS

Tapes (After Robert Earl Davis Jr.)

Having drove a nail

through the dial tone, hon

—Sun gone candied in those

glass-shaped handclaps

JAZZ EDUC-ATOR

Four Colors for the Based God

LONG LIFE SLOW
GROWTH AND PERFECT
COURAGE

GIVE ME THAT LOOK

I'M CALLING
ALL THE WAY FROM
THE END OF THE
SIDEWALK LIKE IT
WASN'T ONLY
YESTERDAY AT ALL
PAST A BUSYARD
INTO NOISE SHOWS

SO STILL IT
IS OUTSIDE ALL THIS
TALK OF HOW MY
WRITING WILL HAVE
CHANGED BY EITHER
EAR'S RINGING'S END

LOST IN THE MOVES

DAILY FLUIDS
FUSED IN THE SYLLABLE-
THINNESS OF PASSING
AVALANCHES NOT
A NEW IDEA UNDER
QUOTIENTS WRECKED
AGAINST IT

EXPELLED INTO
PURPOSIVENESS VS.
MUST I BE SO FUCKED
UP ALL THE TIME

BUT WHAT IF
NOTHING FLOATS UNTIL
APOTHEOSIS ANYWAY

SO ONE'S BAD
EYE'S OLD GLEAM
GOES

BLINK AND IT
CUTS TO UNRELATED
LAST WORDS IN THEIR
REGALIA OF PUFFY
ENUNCIATION

IN FOREGROUNDS
BEYOND AMBIENCE

WHEREAS RHYTHM
BECKONS NO ONE IN
PARTICULAR TO SPELL
THE SAME SOUNDS
FURTHER WAYS AND
AFTER AN ENTIRE
YOUNG ADULTHOOD
OF THIS THE COURSE
OF CORRUPTION IS
PERFECTED

UNLIKE DRUNK
NEIGHBORS WHO
JUST DO IT FOR YOUR

AMUSEMENT WITH
APLOMB NOT SOME
DUMB WRONG WAY
TO WRITE THINGS

REVOLUTION
MADE GROWN WOMEN
AND MEN OUT OF
MY FRIENDS BEYOND
THOUGHT'S LOSSES
MINCING CATASTROPHIC

LET'S ONLY
CALL A BODY WHAT'S
LEFT OF IT

NOT THE THOUGHTS
ABOUT IT NOT THE FEELINGS
ABOUT THEM EITHER

NOT THE THOUGHTS
ABOUT THE FEELINGS ABOUT
THE THOUGHTS ABOUT
THE THOUGHTS

FOR IN ITS DARK
I RAN INTO A MILLION-LEAVED
OAK TREE COASTING LOW
SO FAR INTO THAT DARK
THAT MY EYES DIDN'T GET IT
UNTIL THEY REALIZED
IT'S THE TREE
THAT'S THE DARK

AT HEART TOOK UP
IN LOGIC BLINKING
THANKFULLY OUT
AT PRAIRIE LIGHTS

IT'S A SEALED KNOT
BESIDE THE POINT

WHOSE TYING'S
INTERRUPTED BETWEEN
FIGURES IN EXTREMIS
AND A WORD I'VE NEVER
USED BEFORE IS UP
AGAINST THE SEVERAL
MILLION LIDS ON CANS
OF FACTORY FRUITS
TRASHED THIS BUSINESS
DAY BY MOST FOLKS

WHO'VE LOST TRACK
OF THAT HEART
RATE OR WHO GOT
WHICH INCH OF TURF BOUGHT
BEFORE THE LAST CORD
TANGLED AROUND THE LAST
PHONE CALL CAME
ALIVE AND ATE
ITSELF I'M JUST
GOING UP THE LIST
HERE A HEDGE AGAINST
AUDIENCE REQUESTS OR
MORE ORDERS COME
DOWN FROM CORPORATE

      SYMPATHY FOR
NOT HAVING A CLUE
WHICH SCORCHED EDGE
OF THE WORKFORCE
IS GOING TO GO FIRST
AND JUST CARRYING OFF
YOUR PLANS FROM IT
PULLING THEM OUT
OF THE GROUND

      AS TRAFFIC
FLUTTERS LIGHTLY
NEAR THE BRAIN-
ERASING CLIMAX

OF OUR IMPERATIVE
MEMOIR WEBINAR

AH SHUCKS YOU CAUGHT
ME BOSS I'M ONLY HOLDING
DOWN THIS JOB BY DOING
WEIRD THINGS LIKE KEEPING
UP WITH THE DAILY WEATHER
OF THE CITY I JUST MOVED
AWAY FOREVER FROM

INDOOR VANITIES
UPTIGHT AND COCKEYED
STARING INTO DOORFRAMES
LIKE THEY WERE HOUSEFIRES

IN THE LIMELIGHT
AT THE BOTTOM OF THE LAKE

IT'S ETCETERA
O'CLOCK BEHIND
YOUR MOUTH

WHATEVER HAPPENED

MEANT WE WOULD
BE HERE NOW

FORESTED WITH
PINE AND ASPEN ON THE
GLIDING YEARS HENCE

FORGETFULNESS
WROTE IT

HOLDING THE
PHONE UNDER
CORE-SAMPLE RAIN

AS YOUR AVERAGE
WAVE TAKES VAGUELY
THE SAME TACK AS THE
ONE BEFORE IT

AS REMAINS SHOOT
VIVACIOUSLY FROM ROOTS

AND ERRORS PASS

A TUNE TO SOOTHE
THE RICTUS OF THESE
FINGERS PLEADING
SWEET RELEASE
FROM THE PLOT FIRE

POLYPHONY
RECEDING INTO
DISSONANT GULFS

WHOSE WORLD IS PITCH
MADE FLESH AND WILL
NEVER EXCLUDE US

FOR LIFE IS NOT
EXAMPLES

SO AFTER MANY
PREFACES WE'RE
DRUGGED IN WELCOME
BY A SLACKENING
SYNC BETWEEN AUDIO
AND VISUAL TRACKS

IN AIDED TALKS
THROUGH MINOR
LISTENING SKILLS

I CAN'T STRESS
ENOUGH

ABSOLUTION
DOESN'T MEAN THE
MUDDLEHEADEDNESS
GOES POOF OR THAT TIME
SUDDENLY WINDS UP
AT 100% WITH ONLY
THE MOST SUPPORTIVE
RESIDUE TARRYING
BEHIND

AS ROOT GLOBS
UNDULATE IN TRACE
WINTER'S MEANTIME
ADHESIONS NAMED FROM
EXTRA-CELLULAR WASTE
THAT THINKS IT WOULD
RATHER MAKE SENSE
THAN SURVIVE

I SUFFER FROM
THE PROBABLY COMMON
DELUSION THAT I SUFFER
FROM REALLY UNIQUE
DELUSIONS

LIKE HOW I JUST
KNOW WE'LL BE SHOWERED
WITH SAVINGS IF EVER
AN INSTRUMENTAL
BREAK IN THE CLOUDS
PERMITS

I'LL BE THIS
CLOSE TO STAYING
THE SAME THEN

BUT HEARING
THE ANSWER COME
FROM THE SCREEN OF
OBLIVION WAS SO MUCH
MORE DEGRADING THAN
THE ACT OF POSING
THE QUESTION THAT WE
UNFOLDED OUR ORGANS
AND FLED BEFORE IT
ENDED CATCHING JUST
THE MENISCUS

AS MORNING'S
PEARLED SPILL
SALVES SORROW
AND SHAME

MANY LETTERS
MANY ARTICLES

SMUDGING OILS
AND PIGMENTS

A TOUCH GRACES
MUSIC'S MEMBRANE

A PITCHED PAUSE
WE'D SLEEP LATER
THAN GOD IN

I'LL BE THIS CLOSE
TO STAYING THE SAME
THEN THOUGHT THE
PHILOSOPHICALLY LONG
ODDS ON REBIRTH IN
VERSE OR CERTAIN
CURTAINS IN VERSE

OH SING TO ME
SIGHTS UNTRAINED
FOR I HAVE NO IDEA
TANK DROSS TO
SIEVE THROUGH MY
CHOOSINESS

IT'S MAY AND I
AM ELSEWHERE LOOKING
LONG AT THE SALT-
CLOTTED WATER FALLING
THINKINGLY TOWARDS
THE DEEPEST SURFACE
HIGH AS HELL AND TOTALLY
DEVOTED FOR THE
MOMENT TO THIS
IMAGE OF SALT IN WATER

I SAT CAKED IN
GAZES HEADED FOR
AND FROM IT

AS IN HOW THE
DRIVING OF A NAIL INTO
WOOD IS BOTH THE BUILDING
OF THE HOUSE AND THE
HOUSE ITSELF

YET DEPENDING AS
EXPENSIVELY AS EVER
FROM MY OWN PROOFS OF
PURCHASE HAVING HAD IT
WITH LYRIC'S GORGEOUS
IFFY-NESS

AS TRUCULENT
AND UNRELIABLE AS
I WAS AS A KID

HENCE ALL THE
SOLO PROJECTS

THOUGH SLOWLY
THEY TOO LEAVE ME
COWERING IN THE FACE
OF THE MOST TOTALLY
UPLIFTING WORLD MUSIC
COMPILATION ALL HITS
SUNG BY THE ORIGINAL
ARTISTS

GIVING ME THAT
LOOK THAT SAYS "THIS
IS STILL THE POEM?"

FOUR COLORS
DEVOUR THE MODEL
DAWNING METHODICALLY

WE SEE ITS SCENES
TO FLAMES SO THAT SUNS
MIGHT END IN THEM

YESTERDAY
AT CRISSY FIELD IN
THE OPEN WIND WITH
DOGS AND FRIENDS THEN
THE FRETTED DRONE
OF WINTER AT THE PACE
OF GROWN SKIN

THE WORLD BELIEVES
WHAT I TELL IT THE EARTH
AND SEAS NOT SO MUCH

HUH WELL

DON'T WE ALL JUST
WANNA SLOUCH INTO
CIRCUMFERENCE WITH SOCKS

ON SCOOTING ACROSS
ART'S CARPET

TO TURN THE FLOOR
TO LAVA

AND SLEEP THE SLEEP
OF THE TINCTURELESS

AND WAKE UP READY
TO TAKE THE NAMES
AWAY FROM THINGS?

EVERY CRAZY-MAKING
GAME MADE OF EQUAL PARTS
STRATEGY AND BLIND CHANCE
MUST HAVE ITS OWN WORKING
DEFINITION OF <u>ACCURACY</u>

OH I BOPPED ALONG
AS THE TIME SIGNATURE
TURNED OUTSIDE IN

CUT FLOWERS AND
TAPE WARP AND TAPE
WEFT AND TAPE WOOF

MAY CHANGES OF HEART
SPILL EVERYWHERE
AND GREENS PILE HIGH
IN THE COOKWARE

FIND THE HANDLE
ON THE BRIEFCASE
FOR SOME REAL
FIELD EXPERIENCE

"NO SECRESY IN ART"
—WILLIAM BLAKE

*

Accuracy

Wake and repeat.

Every day I'm asleep.

Where letters are

to put an end

to what makes a mark,

many exceptions

steady together

steps away, addressing—

probably still out there;

one learns to rake

the nerves away

along drones of décor,

swarm of overtone

waving its receipt around;

calls flood the floor...

Jammed into

such rinds,

who wouldn't like

to pry into

that bit of

whatever's left blank,

something for endeavor

to detach to,

knowing how time grows

at both ends,

how awe can't guide it out.

A shame, we say—

Nothing stands in my way

except this nothing

standing in my way!

Meanwhile hairs fall;

a body sends a ball

down a hill;

those ads in the stations,

they know we're not home;

that steel never sees

the light of day

bruised through it,

a clarifying agent wherein air—

much of which is lust

for loss or some

such worseness—

cups the window,

cozens the door...

Lately I've been

busy, affixing to

our margin this

hardly-ochre glow

of trees at streetside

and trying not to think

of margin vanity, how

miscast I clearly was

in my own audience,

myself a tic of drag-

and-drop automatism;

having spent the last

few days in the present's

grainy source meal—

no explanations,

tons of rain, a cold

dose of chlorophyll

in flashes of lavender

yawning in a city park

whose lights are off

from budget cuts

ten miles from this spot—

I'm all back and forth

and calling *systolic*

how fast clouds grow,

how far the dead go,

as do the living in

their bodies of rules

of thumb whose hurt

never grudged

an object its rust.

Don't waste away

on depths and

their surfaces,

on surfaces and

their depths, it said—

Of course it's forever;

how else would it end?

There's a call spreading

over cold clouded water—

static hangs from

every eyelash;

a sky's blunt litany

clotting the void so as

to fill pages and later

empty them,

a hole through the theme—

All the bells turn around.

It takes a lifetime

to clear a name.

—blind loss and weird

fury after which our

gorges rose, not waiting

for anything, no

shadow down the frame;

what I meant was

insufficient, but by what?

"One says it's raining not

to mean that the rain is

performing an act but rather

that something is happening":

bikes bunching up along

the doggy promenade;

two clocks two minutes

off in the same room;

or probably there's no

such fiction to dredge for

definition in, and all night

watching ice not melt to red

in delta form solvency,

congealing in sieves;

I rise as a river does

when crossed? Accuracy

doesn't bludgeon me,

a shivering interval.

I know the smell

of rain's name:

Petrichor: *petra*, stone

+ *ichor*, the glassy stuff

that runs in Greek

gods' veins.

Another week then.

No one seats us.

I've never heard the truth

but keep it in heaps

nonetheless, thinking

there'll be chances

down the road, thinking there's

time in the world...

But time is between blood

types at the moment.

Appendages are enraged:

this notch in the saw,

this slant in the hand,

some slim inch of surface

not very well buried

(having never

been better),

blank as tracing

paper stacked

opaque and hardly worth

its weight in second

hands—dotting

a prior horizon—

Induce and yield.

I'm trying!

For what is a thread

intended?

A light dies

so I buy it, as it strays

from whatever

else of itself's left;

a border's

broader than

its core;

my shadow

works hard, I'm alive

as an Earth's worth

tempts the calendrical distance;

stretched too thick,

waking's vacancies

recede intact,

remote but fiercer for it.

*

OUT OF SHAPE
AND INTO POSITION

THE POEM FAR
FROM BEING FOUND
APPEARS THERE NEARLY
NOT MISSING

SO IF THE STITCH
THAT SEPARATES TWO
DOTS GROWS DO THE
DOTS GROW

IS THAT WHAT'S
BETWEEN ME IN THIS
LUMBERED SUNLIGHT

HALF CUT OUT OF
ITSELF HALF LODGED IN
ITS SOLACE HALF BACK-
GROUND WALL BAUBLES
HALF LEFT ALONE IN A
PLACE OF NEED WITH
ITS LITTLE CAP OFF

WEARILY MY
DEAREST THIS SPOKE
AT YOUR TIGHT-
ROPE'S LIP

ALTERNATION AND
SAMENESS ALTERNATION
AND SAMENESS

IT'S CRUEL AT
THE WINDOWSILL AND
DRENCHING EVERYWHERE
ELSE SO THE SLEEPER
KEEPS GETTING NOT
CAUGHT UP WITH THEIR
INVENTORY

LET'S SEE

THERE'S DOWN TIME
AND BUSY TIME AND
THAT'S ALL THERE IS

IN A FRETWORK OF
CONVINCEDNESS RODE
MY REPUTATION LIKE
A NATION-WAVE UP
TO THE WRONG HOUSE AND
OUT WITH THE RECTIFYING
ROLODEX OF "IT'S NOT
LIKE OTHER PEOPLE
EXIST JUST IN CASE
OF EMERGENCIES"

AND JOKES FOR ALL
OCCASIONS EXCEPT
THIS ONE

A LOT OF SMALLISH
EARMARKS REALLY GUMMED
IT UP AND WE ARE OUT OF
HERE FOR LONG-PLOTTED
HOLIDAYS NOT MISSING OUT
ON WHAT LIFE HAS TO
AND IN FACT MUST OFFER
SINCE LAWS WERE PASSED

IN OUR FAVOR TWO
SUNDAYS AGO

AS PEACHY BALLOONS
FELL ABOUT OUR CASTED
BODIES

AND DOESN'T
EVERYBODY NEED
A NEW ONE ON A SUNDAY
WHEN NOVEMBER
TURNS INTO YOU

SCREEN TWISTING
IN THE SLEEP SIGNAL
DRIVEN TUNEFUL AS
QUARTER-BIRDSONG
OUT OVER ACREAGE
IN RETURNING AIR
STEEP AS A HILL FULL
OF SOULS WE LEARN
"GEM-TACTICS" VIA GREEN
ASCENSIONS IN COMMON
LEFT OUTSIDE THE ACT OF
HAVING WRITTEN IN AN
OPENING OTHER THAN
THE PRESENT'S DRESSY

INFLECTIONS ANYONE
FEELS WEREN'T HERE
BEFORE OR AT LEAST
NOT IN THIS ORDER'S
WHAT I MEANT WHEN
I GOT TO THE ENDGAME
IT WAS JUST A BUNCH
OF SIDELINES MAKING
IT OFFICIAL ALL ART
IS HELPLESS BEFORE
WISDOM AND LOVE

A TRANCE BETWEEN
EXTRACTS

WHEREAS WE LOOK
OUR WORST REFLECTED
BACK TO US IN MIRRORS
WROTE TOLSTOY IN
WAR AND PEACE

WHEREAS A DESIRE
TO APPEAR COMPLICATED
IS AT THE ROOT OF
MOST FORMS OF FATUITY
WROTE HENRY JAMES
IN *THE TRAGIC MUSE*

OH I FEEL A BLOG
POST COMING ON ON THIS
SIDE OF MY SPINE A BURNT
SHIVER COUGHING DOWN
LUNGS OF ASPHALTED
VITAMIN POWDERS AND
FEELING LIKE A HOT CLOAK
IN A STEAM ROOM AWFUL
IMAGE BUT YOU'VE GOTTA
EMPTY THE BATHS SOMEHOW
AND EXEUNT THAT
HALCYONIC FUNK

LAST PAGE REASONS
ALWAYS WIN

AND YET IF JUST
GIVING UP IS FUCKED
WHO WILL TAKE IT
FROM THE WRONG HANDS
AND JUST LOVE US
ON OUR WRONG FARMS

AS FROM THE DEPTHS
OF THE BACK OF THE ROOM
A SONG BELONGING TO YOUR
KARMIC ARCHIVE'S TRYING

LIKE A CAR ALARM TO BE HEARD
THROUGH THE PAPERWORK
AND DOESN'T WANT TO HEAR
ABOUT WEIRD HIRSUTE
PLEASURES SUCH AS OURS

      **THE SOUND
OF PENS FOUR
FEET DEEP**

      OF FREEDOM
IN NOISE

      AS *L'ANGE*
PASSE

      DON'T MOVE

      **I USED TO BE
A FIGURINE ON CAKES**

      ENCIRCLED SOUND
AND VISION IN AN AUDILE
FOG STOPS SHORT OF

FLOODING BLEAK STRENGTH
EIGHT CONSONANTS FOR
EVERY VOWEL CLAMORING
OVERHAUL OVERHAUL
OVERHAUL ITS SPLINTERS
FOUNTAINED IN AND OUT
FOR AS LONG AS THE
CITY KEEPS ITS PIPES UP

    BUT GLITTER
NEVER DIES KEEP IT
ON YOU DON'T WASH
IT OUT TO SEA

    GIVE IT A YEAR
OF WEEKENDS

    THE AIR ELSEWHERE
MAYBE HELD TOGETHER
BY A FIR TREE

    WIND BATTERING
THE WARM FRINGE

    YOU ARE NOT
TOO OLD TO SPEAK

YOU GROW THROUGHOUT
THE WORLD IN CULTIVATED
AND WILD FORMS

BEYOND THE CHALKILY
SUSURRATING DIN OF
"OUR REASONING WAS
STRAIGHTFORWARD"

THIS IS ALL VERY
INTERESTING BUT I HAVE
TO GET ON WITH MY LIFE

WELL PAST THE
NICE PARTS THAT ALWAYS
AGREED WITH US

ON TO THE NEXT
PAGE ONE THINKS AND THEN
OH WAIT YOU'VE BEEN
THERE ALL ALONG

AS NABOKOV WROTE
OF GOGOL'S "OVERCOAT"
GRADUATING DRASTICALLY

TO ASPECTS OF "THAT SECRET
DEPTH OF THE HUMAN SOUL

WHERE THE SHADOWS
OF OTHER WORLDS PASS
LIKE NAMELESS AND
SOUNDLESS SHIPS"

OUT OF NEAREST
DISTANCES BETWEEN
TRANSCENDENCE AND
PROXIMITY THESE SALMON-
TO-TYPICAL CLOUDS
THAT FASHION AND WILT

AT WHICH POINT
WE CAN MORE OR LESS
MELLOW OUT WHILE
THE SONG FOLLOWS ITSELF
PAST ITS INNER-TREK
ELEMENT SINCE THE REST
JUST SEEMS LIKE BLEAK
RECESS OR WHAT
LITTLE BOUTIQUE
RECORD LABELS DO

SOUPING UP AN
ALBUM THAT WAS MADE
IN THE CD ERA AND WAS
75 MINUTES LONG AND
NOW THEY CUT IT HALF
AN HOUR SO AS TO SELL
THE THING ON VINYL
AND IF IT'S NOT THAT THEN
IT'S DOUBLEWEIGHT TRIPLE
VINYL IN AN EIGHT-PANELLED
SILKSCREENED CARDSTOCK
GATEFOLD SLEEVE COME
ON IT WAS REMASTERED
FROM CD ANYWAYS AND
STILL I BUY IT

A SLAVE TO TASTE

THE DAY ARRANGES
THINGS SO THAT ONE
CAN JUST UNHUNCH
AND WATCH WHAT'S
COVETED FLOAT AWAY

BLANKING THINKFULLY

AND SHOOK OFF GOOD
LEADS ON THE CASE THAT
MADE MY NAME

BUT A QUICK SOLDER
AND CAUSALITY'S BACK
FROM A LONG DATA
STORAGE CONFERENCE
WHOSE TAKEAWAY IS "BLINK
AND YOU'RE DEAD" AGAINST
A SCRIM OF FOREIGN
SKIES IN THEIR TYPICAL
DISTANCES PLANNING
URBAN PLANS AMIDST
VAST ZOMBIFICATION

SUBJECT MATTER
SUCKED BACK TO SOURCE
CODE AT BEHESTS
OF DESCRIPTION'S
LINEAGES ACTING LIKE
EVERY LAST ITALICIZED
SCRAP OF APPROACHING
REALITY'S "THE ONE
THAT GOT AWAY"

CALL BACK BEFORE
NOON CALL BACK AFTER

NOON LOOKING FORWARD
TO THE RETURN PLUNGE
THROUGH AURAS OF
ACADEMY REAM SLUDGE
CLOTTED ARTWORKS
IN THE FORM OF SOME
SORT OF GET-TOGETHER
AFTER THE GALLERY THING
TO WONDER WHAT IT IS

AND I DO WONDER
WHAT IT IS ABOUT ME THAT
KEEPS PAIN THE SAME
THING EVEN AS OTHER
PAIN TAKES ITS PLACE

IT'S THE DIFFERENCE
BETWEEN STOP AND END

A TOKEN ORDER
PLACED JUST TO SHOW
IT CAN BE DONE

THERE IT SITS
SOAKING ITS OWN VOID UP

HARD TO MAKE ALL
THE EDGES MEET
AND STILL KEEP
THINGS READABLE LOL

HENCE THE SELF-
RELEASED THING CUT FROM
EXQUISITUDES OF ACCIDENT
IN LIEU OF OLD-TIMEY SUMMER
BREAK APPRENTICESHIPS

ENTIRE BAD TRIPS
ABOUT THE POINT I MEANT
TO WANT TO MAKE IN ITS
CRANKED GAIN OF
WORDS AND DEEDS

THE NOTION THAT
REALITY IS NOT LIMITED
TO WHAT'S REAL CREATES
AN INTERSTICE WHEREIN
THE NOTION OF TRUTH
FINDS SHRILL BLOOM

AND SURE
ENOUGH IT CAME

OR DIDN'T REALLY

AND SURE
ENOUGH IT WENT

THOUGH IT NEVER
DID THAT EITHER

AND THE THING I'D
BE DOING ON A FOLLOWING
DAY THAT RESEMBLES
THIS ONE EXACTLY DOWN
TO A FAINT HALTING AND
REFRACTED ATTITUDE
TOWARDS METHOD HAS
BEEN MOVED TO REGENESIS
BY THE FOUR-DIMENSIONAL
MACHINE DIN THAT
FLOATS LIKE A HORIZON-
BROADENING BOREDOM
ACROSS THIS FILM OF
SPIRIT I'LL CALL DEPTH'S
SURFACE

FELT A PANG OF
OLD SURGERY IN
THE NEW MOVES

YOU TASTE THOSE
STAPLES ROAMING THE
VERY MUSCLE YOU HEARD
THIS WITH TO TURN
AROUND AND NOT
ASSUME THE WORST

YOU THINK OF
THE LAST THING THAT
COMES TO MIND

A CARDINAL
BEAMS THROUGH HEAT
AS MY BODY LIES ACROSS
THE PROPER LABORATORY
BOOTH AMONG MUSICIANS
AND THE FIRST DAY OF
DREAM SCHOOL

SHADE BLEACHED
AWAY

THEN THE MOON IS
ELSEWHERE BOUNCING
OFF OF SOMEONE ELSE'S
SUN

PRESENT PAST
FUTURE BROUGHT TO
MIND BY A SUDDEN
UNCTUOUS BURST OF
TWENTY SIX LETTERS

I DREW UP THESE
PLANS WITH THE SHORT
ENDS OF STRAWS

I EXISTED MY
WAY THROUGH THIS LIFE
ON NOTHING BUT
PROPORTIONS

OH TIME ME FOR
I KNOW NOT HOW
LONG I'M SUPPOSED
TO HAVE STOOD AROUND
IN GLOAMING'S PICKY
DARKNESS

FIRE FIRST

SYSTEM AND
SHAPE LATER

COME ON WE'RE ALL
SCIENCE MAJORS HERE

THERE'S SPECTRA
ENOUGH FOR US YET

CUTTING UP THE
MODERN WORLD'S SURFEIT
OF COVER ART AND
ROUTINIZING LAST THINGS
ACROSS ENTIRE GREATER
METRO AREAS

SO INTO RHYTHM
ONE'S KNOW-HOW
IS COAXED

BUT STILL I MOSTLY
LOUNGE AROUND AT HOME
SIPPING THE CHALICE
OF THE LAST PLAIN PHRASE
KNOWN TO HUMANKIND

TRYING SOFT TO
FIND OUT WHO KNOWS

WHAT AND WHO'S
UNDRUNK ENOUGH
TO SAY SO

DOOM IS NOT THE
ONLY THING I'VE NEVER
SEEN THAT WE'VE GOT
TO CHOMP ABOUT

HAVING SET FOOT
NEXT TO NOTHING
IN A SHARK TANK

THE GOOD
BOOK IN HAND

AS CONSCIOUSNESS
SUDDENLY DOESN'T QUIT

YOU'VE HEARD
THIS EVERYWHERE ELSE

WHEN SEVERING
IS THOUGHT THOUGHT IS
NOT SEVERED

CAT SPOOKED BY
DEMON SPRINKLERS
AT DAYBREAK THEN BACK
TO THE PERCH

A THOUGHT IS NOT
THINKING THINKING IS
NOT THOUGHT AND WHILE
I'M DISORDERED LIFE FILES
DOWN THE NIB

AND SURE IT HURTS
TO HEAR IT TOLD IN A
CERTAIN WAY LADEN WITH
TRICKIEST SYMPATHIES

BUT MIND FLIES AND
I'M OFF TO THE DANCE

SCENE OF DAWN
THICKENING IN LINKED
COLLECTIONS GLIMPSED
THROUGH THE EXPIRATION
OF MY MEMBERSHIPS
BETWEEN COMPETING
WEED DISPENSARIES AND

PUBLIC-SPEAKING CLINICS
THAT CLAP AT WHAT
LEADERS IN THE FIELD
CALL COHERENCE

BUT I AM FOR MORE'S
VIOLET FRINGE

IF A MIND COULD JUST
TURN LIKE A WRIST

LUSTFUL AT WEEK'S
END ONLY TO BE SHOWN
AROUND THESE HOUSEHOLD
HEAPS OF TRINKETS LEFT
ON THE CURB BY SOME
REAL GOOD PEOPLE

YAWNING WITH
NERVES IN THE AETHER
OF A FOURTH EDITION
WELDED TO LEDGES
AND SPLASHING
ORDERS AT DUST

THOUGH WE'VE
ONLY TO BE THE SOLES OF
OUR FEET ACROSS FRIGID
COALS STREWN IN THE
SHADOW OF ANOTHER
TIME ZONE BY THE LIGHTS
OF BRAINDEADLY DIPS
AND SPIKES MARKING US
AS UNREAD IN ABEYANCE

ADVANCED COACHING
NOTIONS CROWD THE
PANEL PRESENTATION

WHY CAN'T WE ALL
JUST GET IT WRONG

PLAINLY YOUR
CHAFF GOT THRESHED
BY THE HASSLE OF HAND-
LETTERING WITH NOTHING
BUT AN INFANT'S TONGUE

THIS IS DUMB
DUDE

BUT YOU STOOD
AS AN UNDERSTOOD
DUDE WOULD AT GATED
PARKS IN THE GRIP OF
ADMISSION COSTS

UNLIKE A LYRIC
SPEAKER WHO IS READY
TO DIE

CROSSED OUT
AND CROSSED OUT
UNTIL IT'S GLISSANDO

THE BLACKBOARD
CUTS ALONG THE
WHITEBOARD CLOTS

BY RAIN'S HAND
MAY ALL RAINGEAR
BE DESTROYED

TIMBRE AND
GRAIN SKY GONE
WHAT GRAYEST

BLUE THERE IS
OR ISN'T OR IS
OR ISN'T

       NOW IS NOT
JUST THE TIME

       SOUNDS OUT
THE HOURS

       TO SWELTER IN
HISS NO MORE

MAN OH MAN

OH MAN OH

MAN OH MAN

OH MAN OH

MAN

Indifference

Home enough in one world,

the unmeant
leading to me—

"Walking away is affective."

Noon's singed
fog's a lost clemency

—hearing this, "in premise"
on high-end equipment

with stitches and swaths.

IMPRESSIONISTIC DEPIC-
TION OF HOW I START TO
MINOR IN THE SCIENCES
AND BLACK MATHS NOT
CONSONANT WITH THE
OLD CHEAT CODES BUT
YOU TRY FINDING YOUR-
SELF CARESSED BY THE
KIND OF PROJECTS ONLY
SOME INSANELY ELITE
TEAM OF EXORCISTS COULD
KNOCK OUT WHILE LIFE
INSISTS ON HOW TO ACT
RIGHT LIKE I SHOULD FEEL
LUCKY TO BE STUCK ON
THIS WORKING VACATION
IN SELF-POSSESSION

Waking Out

Between boredom and shock we oscillate
gods and I

gnawing on the phrase "end to end"

past attraction and resistance
supposition and same pages

a glowing green exit sign busy at its
frigid vigil

posits through another sort of pointlessly
gorgeous coastal afternoon

music by James Ferraro

blinkered and ratchety from half
a lifetime of Norcal cannabis

and the lame doom of state school student debt

$\triangledown$

Excesses of ellipses distinguish
you whose drones opened wide

a mouth to whisper this

boxin' phonemes from hot cogitations
licked insanely by daylight

through senile
and skin-tight distances

skiff grooving unreflective
and bark adrift on trunks

∞

The finest life is turned into insipid fiction
pretty quickly

cloudless blue
upper place wherein sun disappears everywhere

the universe is fine it has its place is
all I'm saying

a piece of coffee linking me to sleep

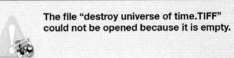

Surroundings

On sundown to sundown
did it never sink in.

There's something missing
on my mind—

what's it like?
What's it sound like?

One ear hears what the other
only chokes out—

hints me there,
hints me home.

IF ONLY I
HAD UNDER-
LINED THE
RIGHT
PASSAGES

Poem

From the top of its heart
in unclouded dark
I stood on sinking feet

The margin gone
out of earshot
half a page across

Whose pause protrudes,
works and breaks,
a hoax of near and far

A lick of calm
trauma where note
and light meet

Where plot holes
grow bigger than
the plot itself

If beauty may
be most of what
is less in place

Its genome's
fibrous surface
flailing outward

From skies, struck wisps
gauze shade or cloud
rows of parked cars

I've painted myself
a corner and can't
get into it

In which I shed
the image,
fake labyrinth

with a real exit

THIS ARGUMENT IS DEEP ENOUGH

Over Noise

Here is my scarcity, a thing of great repairs; here's its
parergon sucked from museum clouds. Stop here and then,
in an ear-ringing excess of derelict air, wherever's left.

Here comes a querulous race to the death where the track
slips up and we quit in the distance. Here appears an up-
date on the past-to-cash ratio, post-consumer recidivism
interests set spinning in the dark crowd so you don't move.

Here's nothing to it.

Churlish inner problems only captured in truer words
never spoken:

that's the trouble around here?

Here goes the cure-all that was my lurid ardor, the curious, worrisome, mind-in-creation-is-a-fading-coal fraud we raised in my defense. Told it was of the essence—

Here (related) is the crease in history where I tuned a knob and the scientific method shrieked apart. My license, twice stolen! Here's a bank between hands.

Here's a blank tape of a bank between hands, here is resonant combustion, here's the engine it ruined.

Back up.

(—that the body clots with presence because pressed to reason sense from it—"it" a massive fragment of infinitesimal complete works—

who are you as opposed to you? Here as opposed to where?

Purposes, likelihoods, difficulty generalizing, scripture, cash back, struck bells, a word for it, a third of it, wetted lenses, tethers, membrane and field, a vague and hopeless sort of fame in one's own time, dying plants from the flea market, "skin flashing to wished-for disappearances," store credit only, and from myself always the same shed light in here, same street and residence, same plainsong and video rentals, same redactions, same time as it runs out —)

Over all the lies that floated out of me like prayers rang a
new glass raised by the coated-over world to every corner of
its removable room. A motion tone grasps refracts over noise.

Things could be different out here: a next life left uncorrected
enough—

Hi you've reached the guest home, the grocery store, the
green freeway, and thrashes shimmer past. We're not here.

HOW CAN YOU TELL